HALLOWEEN

by Charly Haley

Cody Koala

An Imprint of Pop!
popbooksonline.com

abdobooks.com

Published by Pop!, a division of ABDO, PO Box 398166, Minneapolis, Minnesota 55439. Copyright © 2019 by POP, LLC. International copyrights reserved in all countries. No part of this book may be reproduced in any form without written permission from the publisher. Pop!™ is a trademark and logo of POP, LLC.

Printed in the United States of America, North Mankato, Minnesota

082018
012019

Cover Photo: iStockphoto
Interior Photos: iStockphoto, 1, 5 (top), 5 (bottom left), 5 (bottom right), 15 (top), 15 (bottom left), 17, 19 (bottom left); Shutterstock Images, 7, 9 (top), 9 (bottom left), 9 (bottom right), 10, 12, 15 (bottom right), 16, 19 (top), 19 (bottom right), 20; Pacific Press/LightRocket/Getty Images, 11

Editor: Meg Gaertner
Series Designer: Laura Mitchell

Library of Congress Control Number: 2018949957

Publisher's Cataloging-in-Publication Data

Names: Haley, Charly, author.
Title: Halloween / by Charly Haley.
Description: Minneapolis, Minnesota : Pop!, 2019 | Series: Holidays | Includes online resources and index.
Identifiers: ISBN 9781532161971 (lib. bdg.) | ISBN 9781641855686 (pbk) | ISBN 9781532163036 (ebook)
Subjects: LCSH: Halloween--Juvenile literature. | Holidays--Juvenile literature. | All Hallows' Eve--Juvenile literature.
Classification: DDC 394.2646--dc23

Hello! My name is

Cody Koala

Pop open this book and you'll find QR codes like this one, loaded with information, so you can learn even more!

Scan this code* and others like it while you read, or visit the website below to make this book pop.

popbooksonline.com/halloween

*Scanning QR codes requires a web-enabled smart device with a QR code reader app and a camera.

Table of Contents

Chapter 1

Halloween

People wear costumes. Jack-o'-lanterns sit outside. Kids carry bags or buckets filled with candy. It is Halloween.

Watch a video here!

Halloween happens each year on October 31. People celebrate with costumes, candy, and decorations.

Decorations are most often in black or orange.

October

Mon	Tue	Wed	Thu	Fri	Sat	Sun
						1
2	3	4	5	6	7	8
9	10	11	12	13	14	15
16	17	18	19	20	21	22
23	24	25	26	27	28	29
30	31					

Chapter 2

All Hallows' Eve

Halloween is also called All Hallows' Eve. Many different cultures celebrate the holiday. They have contributed to how it is celebrated.

Learn more here!

ancient burial site

But All Hallows' Eve started in ancient Europe. People in Great Britain and Ireland celebrated it.

They said November 1
was the start of winter. They
celebrated the night before
on October 31.

People believed ghosts could come alive on All Hallows' Eve. They lit **bonfires** to scare away bad spirits. Some people wore masks to hide from the ghosts.

Chapter 3

Spooky

Today many people wear spooky costumes on Halloween. This follows the All Hallows' Eve **tradition**. People may dress up as ghosts and monsters.

Learn more here!

People also set up spooky decorations on Halloween. Some have black cats and cobwebs in their yard.

Others have skeletons
and gravestones. Some
people carve scary faces
on pumpkins.

Chapter 4

Celebrations

Not all people wear scary costumes on Halloween. People dress up as princesses, superheroes, and more!

Complete an activity here!

Many children celebrate Halloween by trick-or-treating. They go door to door and shout, "Trick or treat!" They fill their bags with candy.

Many communities also have Halloween events. They have festivals and haunted houses.

Making Connections

Text-to-Self

Have you ever celebrated Halloween? What did you dress up as?

Text-to-Text

Have you read any other books about holidays? What did you learn?

Text-to-World

Halloween comes from an old tradition called All Hallows' Eve. How has the tradition changed over time?

Glossary

ancient – something from a long time ago.

bonfire – a large outdoor fire controlled by people.

culture – the ideas, lifestyle, and traditions of a group of people.

jack-o'-lantern – a pumpkin that has been hollowed out and carved with a face.

tradition – a belief or way of doing things that is passed down from person to person over time.

Index

Online Resources

popbooksonline.com

Thanks for reading this Cody Koala book!

Scan this code* and others like it in this book, or visit the website below to make this book pop!

popbooksonline.com/halloween

*Scanning QR codes requires a web-enabled smart device with a QR code reader app and a camera.